# THE PORTAGE POETRY SERIES

Series Titles

*The Walk to Cefalù*
Lynne Viti

*The Found Object Imagines a Life: New and Selected Poems*
Mary Catherine Harper

*Naming the Ghost*
Emily Hockaday

*Mourning*
Dokubo Melford Goodhead

*Messengers of the Gods: New and Selected Poems*
Kathryn Gahl

*After the 8-Ball*
Colleen Alles

*Careful Cartography*
Devon Bohm

*Broken On the Wheel*
Barbara Costas-Biggs

*Sparks and Disperses*
Cathleen Cohen

*Holding My Selves Together: New and Selected Poems*
Margaret Rozga

*Lost and Found Departments*
Heather Dubrow

*Marginal Notes*
Alfonso Brezmes

*The Almost-Children*
Cassondra Windwalker

*Meditations of a Beast*
Kristine Ong Muslim

Praise for
## *There is a Corner of Someplace Else*

"Steeped in the culture of the Pacific Northwest, Camden Michael Jones's poetry is soothing, startling, tender, moving and insightful. Here are the honest testimonies of the mischievous boy, dedicated teacher, firefighter, historian, husband, outdoorsman, and mindful poet. We find an authentically lived present and a deeply examined past—a rich collection, indeed."

—Henry Hughes
author of *Back Seat with Fish*

"*There is a Corner of Someplace* by Camden Michael Jones brings a fresh, varied voice to the contemporary poetic conversation. Each of its four sections presents a distinctive perspective and topics; each poem offers a personal experience—that we all share. Jones uses deliberate language to say spontaneous things; this is not common. It is refreshing. 'Standing lookout...' presents the fear of fire's devastation better than any other poem I know. The entire section 'Exploration of that Veil' illuminates things passing with honest, simple beauty, perhaps the most difficult voice to maintain in such poems. A very worthy book."

—Marjory E. Lange
author of *Telling Tears in the English Renaissance*
Western Oregon University

"Camden Jones' poetry celebrates the local. These poems are anchored to the beauty of the proximate—from the landscape surrounding Jones' home in the Pacific Northwest to the intricacies of family relationships. Earnest and thought-provoking, this collection is a joy to read."

—Ryan Topper
Associate Professor of English
Western Oregon University

"Camden's versatility, not just as a poet but as a human being, shines through in this collection. Steadfast, calm, and calloused, yet tender and playful. His empathy and respect for the world around him radiates through his work. I return cleansed by flame and with a new appreciation for this Corner that I call home."

—Bryce Fowler
Condon Public School
Condon, Oregon

"Infused with a perspective hard-earned, Jones offers engaging recollections and thoughtful explorations of the world from a life well-lived. Through intimate and honest emotional connection, this collection of poems offers a new lens to view our relationships, mortality, and the world around. These stories serve as a valuable reminder regarding what is real and relevant around us."

—Ryan Forcier
Field Service Engineer
Portland, Oregon

"The West is not always soft, but its allure is timeless... and its lessons endless. Through his unique perspective as a wildland firefighter, teacher and dreamer, Jones untangles the forces and experiences that are ever shaping the West and the lives within it. Stories of life, growth and nature have an undercurrent of nostalgia and a presence that honors relics of the past. Glimpses of his lived experiences give voice to unspoken truths of struggle and stillness in balance; that conflict, which shapes who we are, connects us to a place, community, and heritage."

—Lucas Evans
Engineer, Wolf Water Resources
Portland, Oregon

"As an Oregonian no longer in Oregon, reading *There is a Corner of Someplace Else* brought me home. Home isn't a city or landscape. It is all the little details that Camden notices, remembers, and reminds us to look for in each and every moment."

—Connor Kelly
Salida Montessori Charter School
Salida, Colorado

"Set against the backdrop of rural Oregon, this collection explores wilderness, loss, and everyday life. With beautifully composed poems and vignettes, Jones encapsulates the wonder, breadth, and divinity of these topics. I was immersed in the moments he shares with us. I found myself reflecting on these stories of youth and maturity, life and death, long after I finished the book."

—Chris DeHart
Data Scientist, RealPage
Bend, Oregon

# There is a Corner of Someplace Else

Poems

**Camden Michael Jones**

Cornerstone Press
*Stevens Point, Wisconsin*

Cornerstone Press, Stevens Point, Wisconsin 54481
Copyright © 2023 Camden Michael Jones
www.uwsp.edu/cornerstone

Printed in the United States of America by
Point Print and Design Studio, Stevens Point, Wisconsin

Library of Congress Control Number: 2023937896
ISBN: 978-1-960329-05-9

Cornerstone Press titles are produced in courses and internships offered by the
Department of English at the University of Wisconsin–Stevens Point.

DIRECTOR & PUBLISHER    EXECUTIVE EDITOR
Dr. Ross K. Tangedal       Jeff Snowbarger

SENIOR EDITORS
Lexie Neeley, Monica Swinick, Kala Buttke

PRESS STAFF
Grace Dahl, Zoie Dinehart, Kirsten Faulkner, Brett Hill, Catriona Scheinost, Maria
Scherer, Arianna Soto, Chloe Verhelst

*To my wife, Jessica, for all the things*
*and for raspberry rituals*
*and for hidden friaries*

# Contents

# The West

# The West is soft, sometimes

## I.
There are caterpillars
on the railroad tracks
on my boots
in the grass;
they hang from the trees—
little fruits, animated apricots
fuzzed and ripe—
bodies wet with dew
they writhe against the dawn.

## II.
There is a cattle branding today.
They, the tanned folk
on once-wild ponies,
ride into the fields
to gather in the shaggy beasts.
There are a hundred head, or so,
mamas with babes
still at the tit, some,
and they shuttle
through the gates
with dogs and horses
and people on all sides.

## III.
The stream that flows by the corrals,
channeled deep and dry further up
but sodden and fanning here,
is choked.
Tires. Fence posts.
Rail steel. Barbed wire.

Glass bottles whole and broken.
Bones enough for a hundred cattle,
it seems, jumble the streambed.

IV.
The sun makes its first appearance
of the day, rising bold
above the hills in the East.
It—*he? she? stoic wife*
*or fabulous husband to Luna?*
the sun does not flirt with dawn,
but softly commands day to be;
and it is so.

V.
The cattle, once rounded,
engage in a pastoral ritual
of self-idolatry; they low,
their voices harsh and brutish,
and each effort rattles in the valley
as though each echoing iteration
drawn from the throat
might be heard by one on high
and release their young
from catching ropes
to the fore- and hind-feet,
might scatter efforts to tag
and vaccinate,
might quench the hot iron
coming in to sear
the left flank.
Working them with ropes
of rawhide and hands of calluses,
we answer their form of prayer
with one of our own,

with sweat and denim,
with full coolers
and a barbeque pit
by the shaded stream.

VI.
The West is soft, sometimes,
on mornings like this.
Even the heat of afternoon
is less, sometimes,
after such a beginning.
We work, fingers tangled in hide
and blood and saliva and bands
and hoof and rope and dirt,
but we ourselves are tangled
in ourselves, the men and women
surround, in the sound of water
wending its way and the scent
of hardwood briquettes,
in the sinking into each breath,
in the forgetting of else
but the next calf,
in being a multiplicity.

# Consider the Salt Cedar

*Instead of the apes leaving the trees, the trees left the apes*
                                        –Amadeus William Grabau

Consider the Tamarisk—
the Salt Cedar, that small tree
of Europe and Asia, the way
it grows outward and upward,
reaching, fibers stretching
for the sun and rains,
and the fresh, raw wood
fibers sprout racemes
pink five-petaled flowers
hanging bunch of grapes
weigh vines low
in late summer. Consider
invasion through
the American Southwest,
wanton takeover
of the riparian areas,
and oases full of life.

Consider its contradictions:
it may drink from pools of salt water,
in itself a rare tolerance, filtering
the solution through its leaves.
Beneath, salt deposits form
as a barrier to the growth
of other plant species,
simultaneously weakening
the interatomic binding in clay soils,
causing increased topsoil erosion
and the clogging of streambeds.

The Salt Cedar
must be considered
for surviving conditions
few terrestrial plants abide in;
for raising concertina fences,
salt circles to banish all;
for its ruination of its very soil.

Isn't that always the case?
Given time, even the best adaptions decay.

Yet, the salt, both
lifeblood and destruction
of the Tamarisk
must also be considered,
for when the tree burns
in the summer months,
inferno raging through
thousands of acres in a night,
the salt burns a green so brilliant
it aches to watch,
and the Tamarisk
cleanses itself
from these lands
in an act so familiar
there could be human in those leaves.

# A Hummingbird

hovered behind my left ear.
She, female, large and bright
enough to be a paper lantern
robed in greens and blues,
she must have thought
the white plastic
of my hard hat
a flower amidst the smoke.
She revolved around my head,
close in that her wings
swirled a soft exhale against my cheek
and perched on the front rim.

*A breath.*

With a final vibration,
her claws slipped for purchase
and she disappeared into the morning.

# In Eastern Oregon

historic wheat fields
on highly erodible land
are returned to the Earth
fallow
restored to natural grasslands

at the edge of one
sits a harvester, rusted,
sun rot on roof and leather seat
and tired rubber

the machinery hasn't moved in untold
moons and rainfalls,
withstood the floods of '64 and '96
the scorch of July drought
the knife blade of winter winds

it is half-buried in life,
a ship capsizing under waves
of Bluebunch, Yarrow, Sherman Big Blue,
sinking slowly into the Earth
as if the farmer who left it
might be forgiven for disturbing
the land with a gift of iron and wind
rushing through empty frames

perhaps it will be found,
centuries from now,
rediscovered by an archeologist
studying the early farming
practices of the American West,
and perhaps it will reveal
how fleeting, how temporary
the intent to return to the land is

# The Hills above the McKenzie

Younger
I stood on cliff edges
and was light.
I climbed rock walls
to find a breath
in that space between the colors
of the sky.

Younger found footprints
where they shouldn't be,
traced the routes
of homesteaders,
stepped through the envelope
to stay for a time.

The hills above the McKenzie
River flow like the water below,
logging roads cross-stitch
scars under the canopy,
curving over and around
three brothers and a self
playing at panning
in fairy streams.

# My grandmother plants hollyhocks

*Have I told you about*
*my grandmother's garden*
*in the Oregon sun?*

They grew, bulbous and towers,
clustered crowds
to curtain the windows.
Visiting,
my boyish hands were harbingers
of a destruction; casual
down I chopped them
for no reason but to watch hem fall,
heads rattling against dry leaves,
spilling on the dark mulch
dice or cards or seeds
for next year's growth.
Oh yes, I am of regret for bringing ruin
upon her flowers,
and yes, I have restrained myself
from the same
for many turnings of the sun.
But, it is for that
*withholding, a constraining*
without which I would not know
the alternate; I am of
the tidal forces of devastation
and am rebirth.

# The Oregon High Desert as an Opera House

Can you hear these empty spaces?

The alkaline Summer Lake
trembles its aria daily
under July sun,
baked into an orchestra
of brass and strings.

Only the ignorant dare
shout in this place,
dare raise above the echoes
across the dust.
There is not grace in such
as disregards the plains.

The storms tease each other
on a stage blown
by diurnal winds up canyon walls
and down to spread
as a wave over valley floor.

Some of the oldest human remains
in the Western Hemisphere
are here. The caves here
tell of the Late Pleistocene
lake that filled
this valley and carved
hollows into the basalt
ridges with a gentle
hand and time.
The sandals here show
feet that blistered

up Mt. Mazama and raced
the antelope.
This valley
was an opera and the people
had voices
and they too talked
to the wind and heard echoes.

# Esalen Hot Springs

The cliffs along Big Sur
serpentine the white
tides of the Pacific
and there is a trail
>           paved in the red stone
>           that grasps at the heel
>           ask to say *stay*
that descends into a community
called Esalen.

An hour after midnight
we follow our guide's voice
past curtained windows,
fleece-soft in the night,
and step toe-first
into ancient runnings
from a hole in the wall.

There is a history here.

The fire within these cliffs
tumbles against the cuneiform
in your feet, whispers past
the wind-rinsed flesh of your ribs,
and settles in the dimple
of your clavicle as the pools below
fill with salt and moonlight.

Then empty.

Then fill.

Just as they have.
Just as they will.

# Johnsons' Hummingbird Haven

Stands with the sort of grandness
that only two-story homes have,
especially those homes built
on a slight hill so the grassy lawn,
now the dull sunset of cured summer,
slopes in each direction and in winter
becomes a snow park for the grandchildren.

Johnson's Hummingbird Haven
is this sort of home
as advertised by the wood sign
at the driveway entrance
and the SUV parked out front,
stickers showing a grandson
making honor roll
and the university
where their eldest granddaughter
plays volleyball.

It is the sort of home
that has a wood pile out back,
the rows neatly split and stacked
with the precision
of Tuesday morning spent with sawdust
and coffee and worn flannel.
There are no fewer than seven bird baths
strewn across the property,
and twice that of hummingbird feeders.

That is to say,
this is a nice home.

I walk the property with Boles
and make notes;
I wish I could write
*Dear Johnsons,*
*There is much to do*
*and less time before the fire*
*crests the ridge. Your home is safe.*
but instead, I draw a rough map detailing
where sprinkler kits
and three-thousand gallon port-a-tanks
might be best placed.
I plan its protection.

We erect sprinklers on wood posts.
We dress outhouses and the main building
in structure-wrap. We watch
the flames lick the trees above
and weave through a forest of bird baths
and hummingbird feeders
under a red sky.
We drive away
and hope we have done enough.

## The Yukon appears before me

Alaskan swamps suck to polish
      black leather
      made blacker by wet
from my loggers,
wool socks damp first
at the arch, then toe,
then in through the hollowed
cavity of my heel
      shallow lakes
      around each foot
      turbid particulates
      snag in the sea kelp
      of my leg hair

I slide another wound bundle
of inch-and-a-half hose
down the palm-polished
shaft of my Pulaski,
sink another inch,
and squelch—

—squelch down the firebreak
we cut last week through Black
and White Spruce
until the sodden moss
gives way to river bar
      the Yukon appears before me
she (the river, that is),
she carries the aluminum boats
that shouldn't float but sink
full of gated-wyes and nozzles
and miles of hose, and on this mound
of polyester and river-gray steel
I kneel for the ride.

# The fly rod was older than both of us together

Magpie wings, that windblown spray
flickers between the walls of these canyons
and the same rays that staccato those feathers
whisper through the aspens overhead.
Romero, my boss, had wanted to hike this creek,
part PT
part *get out of the goddamned office*
part the cane rod he pulls from the truck.
*My grandfather's* his response to my eye on his hand
    joining sections
      the old Orvis reel a counterweight
      11 supple feet
      the line hanging from guides
      with the fullness of sunlight.
A few testing swishes and the green line
settles in a lazy way, so deliberate
it's careless, drifts for a few feet,
whirls in a shadowed eddy behind a boulder,
retrieved and cast again
      without so much
            a ripple to mark its place
      the rod rises
and falls,
rod following
hand following
elbow
in smooth overhead patterns calling the wind
and, as if paying homage to the water,
bowing low at the waist.

# Exploration
# of that Veil

## The speech Nixon would have given
## if Apollo 11 had failed on July 20, 1969

*These brave men,*
Dick Nixon would have transmitted
across the nation
on July 20, 1969
if the moon lander
had failed to liftoff from the dust
*will be mourned*
*and their sacrifice remembered*
but of Neil and Edwin
the people would have
traced them in the night sky
as constellations of flesh.

*In their exploration*
*of that veil,*
the words would have trickled
into the lander cabin
stranded on the surface
*these men paved a tomorrow*
*for others*
and waited for the electric click
to signal the end of transmission.
The blood in those lonely bodies
might course in earnest
as though in defiance
of impending starvation
or asphyxiation,
as though a beating heart
could stave off vacuum
and the cold slipping silently in.

*For us who look up at the moon*
*in nights to come*
and feel the weight of above,
we will know
there is a corner
of someplace else
that shall forever be mankind
*let us commend their souls*
*to the deepest of the deep*
*and bid them farewell*
*on their next journey.*

## Dear Mr. Supertramp

In your photo—
  you know the one,
  you were sitting in front
  your bus,
  grinning through
  your ghostly teeth
  clamp to write
  a shorthand apology even shorter /
—did you know then
in that photo
your days would be counted
on calendar pages
torn from that metal frame?
on mere slashes
in your journal
for entries 108-112?
on *beautiful blue berries*
and Alaskan potato seeds?

# Front Seat Stains

We came home from vacation
to find the white feathers
of my tom's face
shifted three inches right
and left to pendulum tumble
in the kiddie's pool
where they stood on water and bumped
against the plastic edges.
His chest, once bold / proud / tall—
was glued to the sharp grass
with maggots boiling from a gash.

I think he tried jumping / flying /
escaping over the fence,
only to fall onto the head
of the nail I hung his feed
bucket from. I like to imagine
        he might have said
        *It wasn't worth it.*

Those avian eyes locked
mine and saw mercy.
In a tarp I placed him
on the front seat
of my '91 Ranger,
drove four miles
into the Oregon desert,
where
        in the headlights
        that made puppet shows
        of big sagebrush
        and hatchet heads,
I took care of my own.

# Store in a Cool, Dry Place

A roommate kept his mother
in a sealed envelope,
waxed,
stored in the back
of his closet
like a stained sweatshirt
too fond of to throw away,
not worn but kept.
I caught him once,
crying, kneeling
before her. He held
her ashes like
she once held him.
Through a gap
in his fingers
I could read
the ink:

> *Date of death: 12/10/17*
> *Date of cremation: 12/12/17*
> *Store in a cool, dry place.*

# Drowned

I nearly drowned once, caught—
      electricity drenched
      and salt-preserved—
in jellyfish nets
of iron and blood and poison.

The waves carried me away
and fire entered my lungs—
      sunburst in flesh,
      on leather-back,
on scars opened and salt rubbed.

A hand, Dad's perhaps,
grabbed mine
      and I awoke
afloat in boiled seafoam
with the same tinnitus as drowned men
ringing in my ears.

## Updates on a Pallbearer

Deb talked to her mom
about me at home; I know
this because at her funeral,
Jenny gave me one of Deb's
shirts bagged in a Ziploc
and sprayed with her daughter's perfume
as if I could forget
what being fourteen smells like.

I met Jenny in a supermarket
just the other years,
and she asked
*How are you?*
but her eyes held empty interest
you see, parents of dead children
ask those questions
to bedroom doors
held open and empty
by skeleton hands
crossing bony fingers
and to seatbelts
that failed at the wrong time,
or were not worn at all.

The crash doesn't kill the body,
you see,
it merely reminds it of its mortality;
it sinks into the desert
and feels the weight
of the vehicle press
into the skin; the crash
reminds the body to give up,
and lying among sage and sand,
it does.

## Apple Tree

Dad cut the apple tree down today.
*It was cracked, broken, dying* he said.
But it was beautiful. Old.

It smelled of the West
of stone foundations
and of light washing
through stained glass windows
wildfire smoke and alkali dust

> Years ago, I wondered
> about God
> while sitting in grass
> beneath, tried one
> sour apple at a time,
> set each aside in turn.

> I filled a jar with dried seeds
> and forgot it on a shelf,
> a gift to a future

Dad cut the apple tree down today
and I breathed sawdust
to fill the gaps between fallen shade
and the empty space
around each seed.

# A Simple Shifting
## of Ourselves

# Self-Portrait as a to-do list
# on a random Tuesday in March

Baby
-start learning sign language
-~~date night with Jess~~
-~~research sex positions for advanced pregnancy~~
-~~find Airbnb in Redmond near hospital~~
-finalize paternity leave

House
-clean out closet (~~bedroom~~ and hallway)
-research how to get a mortgage
-vacuum living room

Self-Care
-~~replace watch battery~~
-~~call pharmacy (blood pressure meds, TDAP)~~
-buy a new pair of running shoes
-start running again
-figure this whole life thing out (a student told me today
they didn't know what to do with their life and my means
of reassurance was to tell them that I didn't know what I
wanted to be when I grew up either. I don't think I ever
will)
-make sun tea

Misc.
-call Delta for reimbursement for cancelled flights
-~~pack for the weekend~~
-research cost to fix broken bumper/call insurance?
-order new fishing tackle before the river opens Apr 1st
-put new line on reel
-~~get grading done~~
-~~schedule meeting with financial planner~~

Grounding exercises for a student
with frequent panic attacks, and myself

*what do I do*
*her arms are scarred hands I sit next*
*to her press my hands into the floor*
*floor press back against the wall*
*and tell her to do the same*
            *breathe slow and deep*
*feel your feet in your shoes*
*and the linoleum is ice*
*on clammy hands legs back*
*and the cold seeps into my chest*
*I am sweaty am shivering*
            *let's get you up and standing*
*feet under and upright*
*and I pick up her backpack*
*and I call her mom*
*and we sit on the steps outside*
*in the full warmth of a late May sun*

# My students ask me to write a poem about them

There is a mathematical argument
that can be summarized as follows:
infinity divided by infinity
is still infinitely larger
than the largest non-finite entity.
Contrarily, a non-infinite number
divided by infinity will yield
results non-infinitely small.
Thus, these non-infinitely small pieces
are infinite in number
implying
within any number lives an infinite.

For my students, the same holds true,
my students, who, in their finite number,
contain an impossible infinity of moments,
kindnesses, cruelties, questions, futures.
They have, for being so young,
suffered infinitely (for they tell me stories
of hard days in ways
I am shattered to know of)
and I watch their small faces
hoping their summers will be spent
at the sea, breathing deep salt breaths
and forgetting the shape of their feet
beneath warm sand.

# Lunch Break in Boise

I found a flock of cranes
clustered in a gravel lot;
they were silent, still,
their grays and reds paint
matte the landscape
behind the jaundice
yellow of the workers
lounging out their lunch;

one fellow, never caught
his name, waved me over
like I'd seen mafia dons
do on TV
　　　*Where you boys headed?*
his voice, rumbles of the diesel
engine of his machinery starting
on icy mornings
　　　*Hell, it doesn't matter.*
　　　　　*You'll be busy all the same.*
*Lunch on me today, son.*

two bills he pushed into my hands,
crumpled and pocket damp,
and slapped my ass in dismissal;
the laughter of the men
shuddered off the steel shells
of those mechanical birds

## What Philadelphia saw
## at George Washington's Funeral Procession

An empty casket borne
by a caisson draped in red and white
rattled through Philadelphia.
Twelve clergy,
disciples of a revolution,
single file having walked
155 miles from Mt. Vernon.
And in front—
two marines wearing black scarves
white gloves escorted a riderless horse
named Blueskin
who carried the general's
saddle, saber, and pistols,
hollow boots reversed in stirrups
to look back on his country
on one final ride.
Nothing, not birdsong nor sobbing
broke the silence
except the rumble of the wagon
and the ring of hooves on stone
coming, then going.
If there were drums, the streets don't recall them.

## On my wife rubbing lotion
## into the backs of my hands

There is wind blowing through the cracks
and the house
whistles with a hollow howl.
Her fingers fold mine, massaging
and manipulating these digits
as a potter might mold
a lump of clay into a work of art.
She pays extra attention to the gaps
between knuckles
where the hair pulls back
and an expanse of skin reveals
layers / let us be layers / let us be
a sum / an amalgam / of all
we have been / of our stories
and changing names /
let us be whole and dethroned /
crownless /
and a simple shifting of ourselves.

## Camping on the Yukon
## with a Veteran Hotshot Crew

On the bank of the Yukon
we tell war stories.
Smoke curls over the hills
behind us and swallows
our campfire boasting.
Steaks on the grate sear
with words dripping
from tongues, oozing
*that was the first time*
*I was shot.*
*The second*
eyes blur with the sulfur
sting of gunpowder,
bearded men tell the circle
*I killed three guys in Afghanistan.*
*I killed four—*
*I killed—*

Confessionals anonymous meetings
on gravel beaches and forest floors,
*Hello, my name is*
we call and respond
in a land without years
to grayling and balding eagles.

The birds listen
and with our words
wind in their feathers, they
dive to dine
on fish, flesh ripped
from silver bodies
left among the rocks
like so much spent brass.

# Two Elderly Men Sneak Out of Nursing Home to Attend Heavy Metal Festival

If I asked you
to sneak out
of our retirement home
in sixty-five years
like we were seventeen
and cosmic again,
would you?

To convince you
I'd say
*Give me the chance*
*to live and let me*
*forfeit the rest*
*as I see fit*
and if attending
the year 2085's
version of Judas Priest
ended my time here,
then I'd have lived
as if I were alive.

I'd say
*Come with me*
because
what would there
be to lose but
a single evening
out of this infinity.

# A Night in the Paisley Community Center

To celebrate another
school year of performances,
the high school theater troupe
spent the night
in the Community Center,
to bond, to play.

Twelve of us
poured paint
on a tarp,
drew portraits
with our bodies,
celebrated our forms
with acrylic
and brushed
the pigments
of desert skies
on the wood-slat walls.

When our games were over,
the drama teacher
let us use his shower,
taking us in pairs
to his house
down the block
to rinse color
from our hair in turn,
waiting in a dark living room
with a smile on his face
and towels in hand

    we reached an arm
    out the bathroom door
    and felt cotton
    and fingertips against still-damp skin

After, he locked himself
in the back room
of that ancient building
and we rolled
sleeping bags
on the worn floor.
We wrapped ourselves
in the touch of classmates,
young, far too young,
loved with other couples,
and were too loud.

These years older, there is still
paint matted in leg hair, the sound
of shifting weight on velvet sofa,
the pressure of ears
pressed against doors
too thin to be soundproof.

# The Mail Plane

### I.

We erect our tents on the hardpack
of the town's airport,
rows of stakes and guidelines
like a fishing wharf in the tundra;
the mail plane comes at one,
an overfull vulture circling above
before looping North towards
the Gates of the Arctic for the approach run.
The landing is
        a front-row rock concert
        where the bassist only knows one chord
        and the drummer is still setting up;
        the tone resonates in the ooze of our marrow;
that is to say, the landing is simple,
drifting low
over alpine fir and spruce tops
before cutting power
and slamming wheels to gravel.

### II.

Yesterday's rain feeds the Yukon today.
Its hands reach for a hard cloud ceiling
and its lows, its troughs call my name,
endless waves in the river center,
arcing with storm energy
and grip strength.

### III.

Other planes come, and go,
and helicopters set down near us.
We play cards in their wind,

drink camp coffee that strains
through the teeth and plugs the gaps;
we watch and we wait
for seats that never come
waiting to leave the airport runway
waiting to fight the big fires.

    IV.
We hear the boats before we see them,
curving around the clay banks
and we line our packs along
their aluminum walls.
We sit in plastic bags
to keep dry of river spray,
I tighten my hat strap
against the breeze
and watch another mail plane
take off. The hardpack vibrates
under the wheels, the engines scream
their one note show,
and the DC-3 sinks off the runway towards
the Yukon—and us—before catching itself,
then slowly, so slowly we can almost raise
a hand and brush the silver belly,
it growls to the North
and loops South towards Fairbanks.

## Conversations in a Tractor

Concentric circles play ring-a-round the rosie,
dancing dust, diesel engine in low baritone,
the tractor cuts 18-foot swathes.

A bee lands on my arm,
soft, staring in its multifaceted way,
bristled legs
entwined with dusty hair.

Do you see the mud where
I floundered yesterday? a day
rusted with waste?
or the blood-spattered
windshield from the fawn
I ran over last week
and fed to the vultures?
the alkali desert and alfalfa
stems drying under August sun?

Or do you see the tobacco spit-stained floor?
rifle in the corner, rounds rattle
with engine noise, steering wheel
picked at by mechanical hands, headphone
cords tangled with boot laces
and baling twine?

Do you see anything
in this tractor
that is itself exactly?

# An Ode to Arthur Dent's Confusion

I, too, know the word Yellow
floating in gray matter
but I don't have the science
to build robots
with synthetic depression
or to cope
with thumbs
that never learned
to aim for space
      (are there statistical
handicaps
      for bad interstellar
      hitchhikers
like in golf)

Is there an encyclopedia
entry for the way
dawn smells on dewy mornings
while lying in a field
outside a pub?
or the thoughts
of sky-bound whales?

I listen to the songs
of this tumbled sea
that is the ground
beneath my back,
and stare at holes
poked in the canvas
above, feeling
for the page edges
of a book

I have yet to write,
feeling for words
that hang the way bricks
never learned to.

What I mean to say,
is that I could go for a pint
or three at lunchtime.

# I see what my own coaches saw

## I.

I am in the front with the driver—
we haven't spoken since leaving town
two hours ago, for we are listening
to the students—
they follow the same pattern
as he and I did during our time
> they group in the back and lend
> small voices to compete with classic rock
> and pop vocalists
> as though each note is the expulsion
> of a body's fatigue at the wearing of the day
> and those clapping laughing
> clipping short words in the mock accents
> of youth acting their real age for the first time
> in many turnings of the moon
semi-trucks pass on our left
and the girls ask them to honk
with dramatized arm motions
while channeling spirits
Shania Twain, Marvin Gaye,
Stevie Nicks ride with us today.
The truckers that oblige my players
—and there are a fair few that do—
those tired men and women of the road
wear grins that match the joy
of my kids      and I from the front
would like to thank them
for their fairy gift of gentleness
freely given with no obligation,
let, or lien.

II.
They give each other nicknames
as children do:
Lebron, Mighty Mouse, Jo (short for Jo Mama)
and a few tell me that when I'm not around
they call me Coach J, Jonesy, Nighthawk.
They can never know
how badly I want them to call me that last,
and I can never tell them
            because how can I?
that, when we stop for dinner
after away games, I will protect them from the guy
with hungry eyes
that hangs outside the McDonald's
and by this I mean claw his belly
and tear him until his insides are outsides
so he can see his lustful soul drain away
and by this I mean kill him,
and that, when I tell them I'm proud of them,
I mean it.
They don't believe me,
I think,
because some, they've never been told that before.
When they lose, I tell them I'm not mad or disappointed
and some, they give me a sad little smile
as if *Yeah, right*
and their double negative is a way to forgive themselves
some, they transgress against their flesh
and some, they wear long-sleeves
and I just want to grab their wrists and never let go
and never let their blood flow down their arms
keep it inside where it belongs
and let it sing and keep you warm
and breathe and fill it with oxygen and more days to
come.

III.
They laugh when they win
and cry when they lose
and in that they are but human
and I
haven't the heart
to tell them
sometimes, even if you deserve          the good,
grief will grip the heart
          and harden you to future          goodness
and that is also human
but it is bravery
to be conscious in remaining open
                    and soft


IV.
We are human, children.
Soft and young inside, do not sow
a hard face. Be fluid.
Be flexible, mobile, able to move
through the days without pain in your joints,
do not groan.
I will be there,
cheering from the sidelines
just as I do now,
waiting, as your coach
and teacher and friend
to celebrate you, each of you,
at the end.

# Hours past midnight on a Washington hillside

awash with glow,
I offer myself to the flame,
reach a hand to sever the link
between heat and branch,
between heat and tree,
absorb along these limbs
the bath, the bathing
of light.
Only what it illuminates—
an owl overhead, silent
on whirling updrafts,
the gray plastic of the UTV
carrying jerries of slash mix,
beards and eyebrows and the steel
of hardened knuckles
gripping tools—some twenty dedicated
servants of the land—are real. We
are aglow ourselves, burnished copper
and bronze and the flush of blood
mere hairbreadths beneath skin
our shadows dance with each other
behind, giants of shadow splayed
across the hill, giants standing still
or walking or throwing fire
from their fingertips, dripping
fire down pant legs until each step
engulfs us further,
we are proof of the fire we carry,
of the dark that light cannot clear
and the sacrifices we leave in our wake.

Write to me.
Yours.

# Fixing a Blown Tire on I-84W

On the shoulder of I-84's
overpass as westbound
enters Portland,
an almond tree
lets down its fruit.

Her petals,
pink, the same as preschoolers
color the sky
and white as the paper
beneath the wax,
tremble in the violence
of Internationals
and Peterbilts,
the same violence
that grabs fistfuls
of my sweater
in intervals.

Jack under, jack up,
lug nuts off after a fight
and this freeway tumbles
in a storm of those flowers
cast off in April-sun,
I am down a layer and sweaty.

Steel wire arcs where sidewall was
and rubber offal marks its death,
traces of black backtrack
those eight seconds of braking
behind.

I am lucky to have stopped
beneath this almond.
It is the only tree in bloom
along this stretch.
Its softness has lessened the day.
Her olfactory embrace deadens
that of axle grease and sun-rot.
I am not afraid of those trucks
passing a wrench-span away.
This is enough, for now.

Theories on the self

Blessed is the *arachnida*, who, in the corner of my kitchen
above a cupboard
builds furniture / *carpenter*
to host the denizens of my home / *fabricator*
and feast upon like a slutty Victorian painting
of Count Dracula bare-chested at a *recline*
and maybe that image is a commentary
on society preying upon the spirit
but maybe / the painter
had a vampire kink
and who am I to judge?

In other news,
I have been waking better lately
and I don't know what to do with that.

Perhaps I am becoming accustomed
to an early schedule, growing, as it were,
leaning into the years to finally fit my personality
like a pair of jeans always hung loose at my hips,
but now, after all, hold me in.
Or maybe, there is something in the dark
that is close / *covered in knit-yarn blankets* /
        *I am the soft wind of a closing door*
*the flicker of dawn through shifting blinds*
        *a shimmering body*
pressed against leather-top desk by the curved arms
of pleather chair coffee gurgle on counter
in belly in mug and warm and soft
perhaps I will let that small friend live
in the corner of this world it has carved out for itself,
if for nothing else than to give company

on these November mornings
where there is something to be cherished;
if for nothing else than the wish for the same for me;
if for nothing else than to have a witness
as the self indulges in the being of a self.

# Dinner

*After Kerrin McCadden*

I love the moment after sitting at the table
in a room, with people I have known—am known
to. We pause, plates dished and steaming,
and we let our shoulders down, which I think
is almost but also nothing like that moment
just before sleep when the breathing settles
and the body twitches to remind itself
of being alive—and maybe we chuckle
a bit in our near-sleep because there is something
inherently embarrassing about being vulnerable—
and maybe tomorrow we will argue
across this dinner table but for now
we let the gentle rattle of dishware speak.

## Standing lookout on a granite butte in Washington while my hometown evacuates due to wildfire

I am not afraid of heights
but I am afraid of falling forever
through the fog of fire, that smoke,
that fingernail in the esophagus,
that pyro-shadow,
of falling forever as if
not watching the rocks below
come closer is worse
than counting down.
Have you ever stood on a cliff edge
and watched the smoke
play its little games
only to get lost
in the moment of looking down?
I linger near the door of *too close*
and tune out the radio buzzing in my ear
to listen to chainsaws chewing
from beneath these lakes of gray
settled in the valleys,
as though not smoke but cloud
and this is not work but play
and my home is not empty and burning

# In 8th grade, we stole my friend's father's truck

We drove the black streets
with daylight dripping
from foggy headlights
upon those liquid nights
so common in the Willamette Valley.

We passed businesses
—the optometrist where
I stared at a hot air balloon
months prior, and
the indoor soccer arena
where we would watch
Byron's father play
tomorrow before lunch
—a deli where
hours before customers
had floated in and out
like buoys on an uncertain tide.
They were empty, now,
this late hour letting streetlamps
have the sidewalks to themselves.

On toes outstretched
for a gas pedal
far enough away
the rubber soles
of my shoes could brush
but hardly press
—I am younger
to reach
the contents
of a top shelf—
I parked on University St.

We ran the pavement
between the school
and downtown
and weaved between
cars between
horns between
those yellow lines
that we walked
tightrope on
as though the wet
in our socks were prayers
to our future selves,
asking forgiveness
for the selfishness of these moments
and for being too eager
to leave them.

## At the kitchen table

Yesterday there were three sprouts
and today there are five
and that is the best magic I have seen
in many passing days
the arugula leaves
are still curled in and down
looped into the soil as if hesitant to let go
reach for the sun
tomorrow they will, bravely
and they will grow just like science
tells us they will but
I would like
to exist, just once in my lifetime,
at the momentary
hairpin unfolding of a new leaf
release spring up
stretch and be enchanted

# In the dark we build

Let me possess you
      as
I am yours to possess
,       this body built
of deadbolts and garden gates
we shall be to the other
as the grass to the fire
      we will consume

until the night
comes
      and we lie here
      naked
in the dark
and build a cathedral
in the space
      between the pillows

## Origami Hands

We sit on white plastic chairs
and watch the rain
wash these streets.
This is not a last meal;
let us origami our hands
and sing our departure songs
to the mirror glass of the sky.

## A roommate from long ago
## used to tie his own flies

He was good too,
spinning wire and tinsel and yarn
into grasshoppers,
mayflies, and worms.
His favorite material,
cat hair,
he would dye using Kool-Aid
and macerate in a food processor.
He used it as dubbing,
using it in fuzzy ants and dry flies.
He filled a box
with these contrived insects,
then two boxes, and four, and more.

He didn't use them. He didn't fly fish.
He gave them away, sometimes to me.

We skipped school and work
to wade into the Alsea and the Nestucca,
him handing me flies
showing me where to cast.

## Self-Portrait as Bram Stoker's
## Valentine's Day Letter to Walt Whitman (1876)

I hope you will consider
this letter, this thousandth
I have written
but the first sent to you,
as an old friend, as a joy,
as an outpouring of my affection.
I trust in a warm reception;
this has lain in my desk
for years, but it speaks
for itself and needs no comment.

What I have wanted to say
is that light is light;
the snowdrifts in the corner
of my building are poetry,
frozen and windblown,
and in them I see hope for spring;
I find myself longing
to meet you on a hillside
somewhere green and fertile,
and we would embrace
as companions who never
lost the love of youth.

Rather, I have wanted to
write this openly
because with you
one must be open.

I am up and dressed,
live here lonesome

sometimes but in spirits
both hearty and good.

Write to me.
Faithfully yours.

# Acknowledgments

When you work on a first book, or any book, I imagine, you inevitably end up with a list of people to thank if publication is ever on the table, but to keep things brief: Jess, above all, for being my muse and sounding board from the first; Rosemary, for being you; Mom, Dad, for being some of the first eyes on many, many drafts of individual poems; Nana, Papa, for the everlasting support; B, A, D, and E, for being the foundation of most of my memories and for being the subject of more bad poems (too gooey, for the most part) than good; Bryce, Ryan, Lucas, Connor, Chris, for being the first reviewers of the completed manuscript; Hughes, Lange, and Topper, for being the best instructors one could ever ask for and for the continued tutelage over the years; and finally, the various members of Cornerstone Press for this wonderful opportunity, including Dr. Ross Tangedal, Chloe Verhelst, Maria Scherer, Zoie Dinehart, the editorial team, and everyone else behind the scenes.

---

Gratefully acknowledged are the following publications, where particular poems appeared in earlier forms:

"What Philadelphia saw at George Washington's Funeral Procession" in *Instapoets* by Augie's Bookshelf Publishing Company (March 2020)

"Store in a Cool, Dry Place" in *Train River Poetry Anthology* vol. 3, Spring, Train River Publishing House (March 2020)

"Apple Tree", "Origami Hands", and "Two Elderly Men Sneak out of Nursing Home to attend Heavy Metal Festival" in *Train River Poetry Anthology* vol. 4, Summer, Train River Publishing House (June 2020)

"The Hills above the McKenzie", "Esalen Hot Springs", and "Front Seat Stains" in *Furious Lit Anthology*, Read Furiously Publishing Co. (July 2020)

"An Ode to Arthur Dent's Confusion" and "The Speech Nixon would have given if Apollo 11 had failed on July 19, 1969" in *Train River Anthology* vol. 5, Fall, Train River Publishing House (September 2020)

"Johnson's Hummingbird Haven" in *Train River Anthology* vol. 7, Spring, Train River Publishing House (March 2021)

CAMDEN MICHAEL JONES is a writer, educator, and wildland firefighter. His work has been published in the *Train River Anthology*, the *Furious Lit Anthology*, and *Instapoets*, as well as in outdoor magazines throughout the Pacific Northwest. He lives in Fossil, Oregon.